SUPER PEGASUS
FAMOUS WOMEN

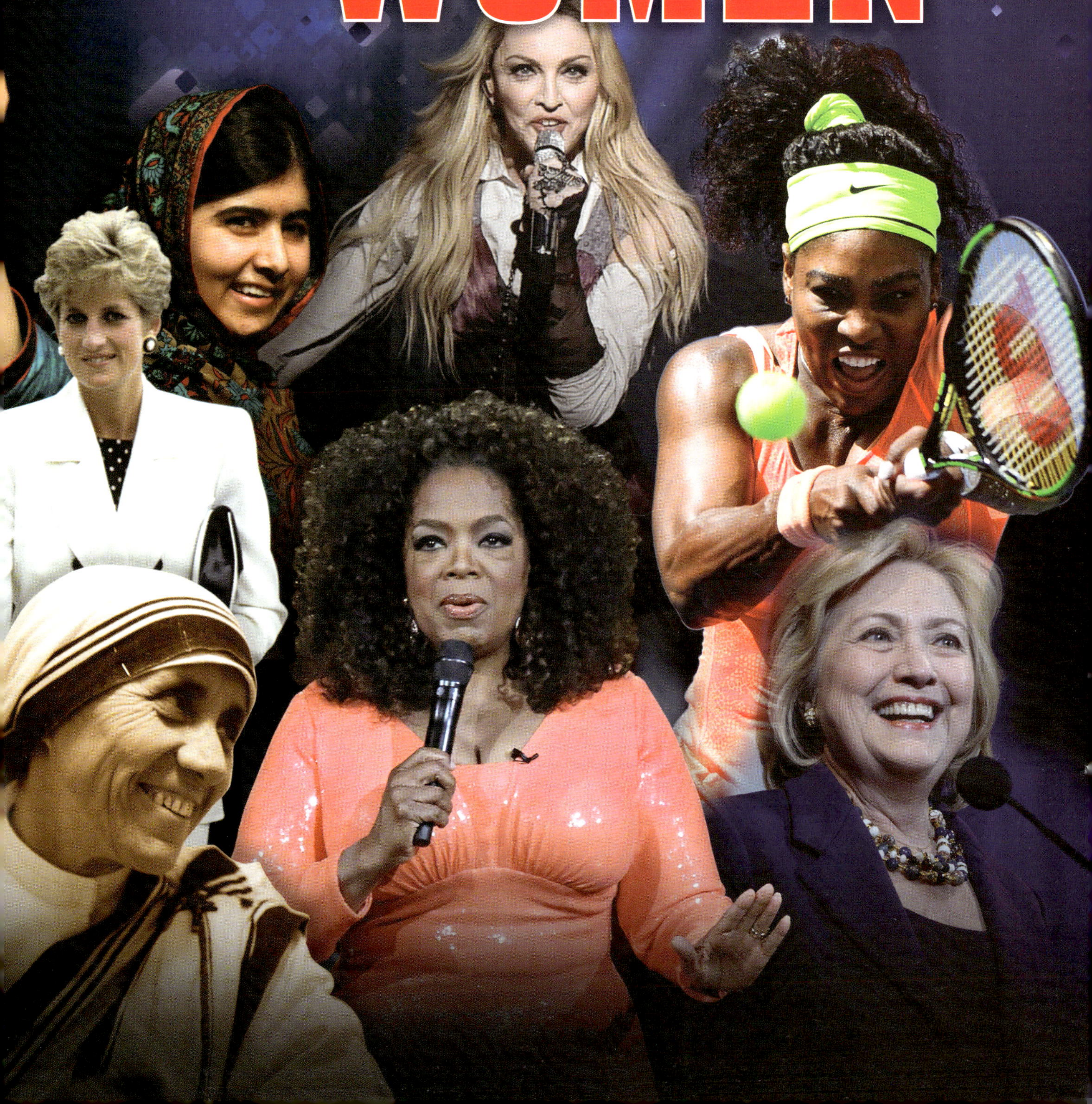

www.pegasusforkids.com

© **B. Jain Publishers (P) Ltd.** All rights reserved. No part of this book may be reproduced, stored in a retrieval system or transmitted, in any form or by any means, mechanical, photocopying, recording or otherwise, without any prior written permission of the publisher.

Published by Kuldeep Jain for B. Jain Publishers (P) Ltd., D-157, Sector 63, Noida - 201307, U.P

Printed in India

All Images © Copyright Getty Images India

Contents

4	Angela Merkel
8	Coco Chanel
12	Hillary Clinton
16	Indira Gandhi
20	Madonna
24	Malala Yousafzai
28	Margaret Thatcher
32	Mother Teresa
36	Oprah Winfrey
40	Princess Diana
44	Serena Williams

Angela Merkel

German stateswoman and chancellor Angela Merkel was born Angela Dorothea Kasner. Her father was a Lutheran pastor and teacher who moved his family east to pursue his theology studies. Angela grew up in a rural area north of Berlin in the then German Democratic Republic. She studied physics at the University of Leipzig, earning a doctorate in 1978, and later worked as a chemist at the Central Institute for Physical Chemistry, Academy of Sciences.

Angela became the first woman ever to lead Germany as chancellor. Angela and the party she chairs—Christian Democratic Union (CDU)—formed a coalition with two other parties in 2005, and the agreement installed her as head of government. Most importantly, she is the first person to lead a reunified Germany after the fall of the Berlin Wall.

A Promising Student

Angela was the eldest of three children in the family. In her youth, Angela was a studious high schooler who excelled in languages, just like her mother. Her command over the Russian language won her a prize-trip to Moscow. Like nearly all other college-bound East German teens, she was a member of the Freie Deutsche Jugend (Free German Youth, or FDJ), the official socialist youth organization in the German Democratic Republic (GDR). However, until then she avoided any political rhetoric and instead chose to devote her time to sciences.

Angela entered the University of Leipzig in 1973. During her student years, Angela worked as a barmaid in a discotheque; and a year before earning her degree, she married a fellow student, Ulrich Merkel. They moved to an apartment with no toilet or hot water in the Prenzlauer Berg district of East Berlin. Renovations of the apartment began as Angela went to work on her doctorate in quantum chemistry at the Central Institute for Physical Chemistry of the Berlin Academy of Sciences. In 1982, her marriage ended in divorce.

Nascent Democracy Movement

Angela earned her doctorate in 1986 and remained affiliated with the Central Institute for Physical Chemistry as a researcher. In 1989, she became involved in pro-democracy groups that were suddenly being allowed to operate in East Berlin and other GDR cities. One of them was Demokratischer Aufbruch (Democratic Awakening). The pro-democracy movement escalated, leading to the opening of the Berlin Wall in November 1989.

Angela's first mentor in politics was Lothar de Maizière, who headed the East German branch of the Christian Democratic Union (CDU). The East Germany Communist Party allowed CDU to operate as a token nod to a multiparty electoral system. Soon de Maizière was named head of a caretaker government and Angela became the deputy spokesperson for his government.

The former East German states were reunified with the rest of Germany in October 1990. Two months later, the first post-reunification parliamentary elections were held, and Angela won a seat in Germany's lower house. The East German branch of the CDU merged

with its West German counterpart that same year, and Angela became a rising star in the party when its powerful leader, German chancellor Helmut Kohl, made her his protégé. In 1991, Angela was made a member of the cabinet as minister for women and young people. In December 1991, she was elected deputy party leader.

Elected Head of CDU

Angela became the first politician from the former East to become a government minister in a newly reunited Germany. In 1994, she became the minister for environment and reactor safety. Later, in 1998, she replaced Kohl as secretary-general of the CDU. She was the first woman to hold the coveted post in party history. In 2000, she proved her mettle further when she ran the party smoothly and became the leader of CDU.

At the time, the CDU was out of power and the opposition party, Social Democratic Party of Germany (SPD), had won the 1998 elections. Gerhard Schröder, then chancellor, was sure to win in 2005 as well. But the German public was thinking otherwise. In parliamentary elections that year, voters gave the CDU a small margin of victory. Schröder refused to concede power, so a grand coalition took place and Angela became chancellor of Germany on November 22, 2005. She agreed to form a government comprised of cabinet members from her own party as well as its counterpart in the southern German state of Bavaria.

During her term, Angela has instituted some sweeping tax cuts for German businesses and has taken Germany to don a more active role as a leader in foreign policy.

Relations with USA

In other foreign policy initiatives, Angela has established more cordial relations than her predecessor with the United States, meeting several times with the then U.S. president George W. Bush. Unlike her predecessor Schröder, she has been a vocal critic of Russian president Vladimir Putin.

In 2007, Angela took over two temporary

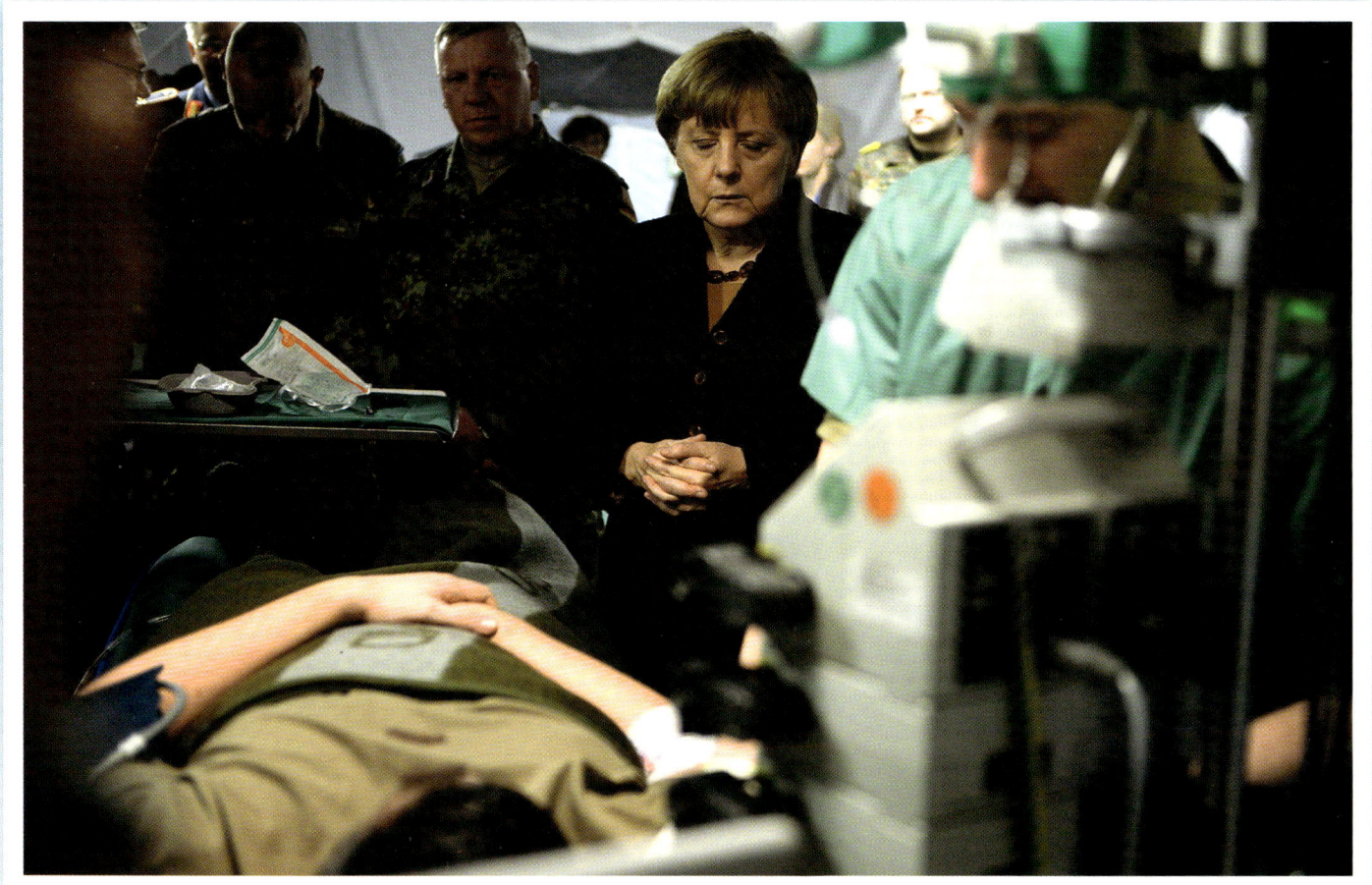

posts in addition to her duties as chancellor of Germany: the rotating presidencies of both the European Union (EU) and the Group of Eight (G8, an international forum comprised of the world's most powerful nations).

Angela earns consistently high marks in public opinion polls. In 2007, Forbes magazine ranked her at the top of its list of the world's most powerful women for the second year in a row.

She was elected to a second term in 2009. Angela again made headlines in October 2013, when she accused the U.S. National Security Agency of tapping her cell phone. At a summit of European leaders, she chided the United States for this privacy breach, saying that "Spying among friends is never acceptable." Later reports revealed that the NSA may have been surveying Angela since 2002. Angela was sworn in for a third term in December 2013 as German chancellor. She continues to wield great power and remains among the most powerful leaders in world politics today.

Fast Facts

Angela has a degree in physics and a doctorate in quantum chemistry. She has worked as a research scientist, as the only woman in the theoretical chemistry section at the East German Academy of Sciences.

Coco Chanel

Famed fashion designer Coco Chanel was born Gabrielle Bonheur Chanel. With her trademark suits and little black dresses, Coco Chanel created timeless designs that continue to enjoy popularity even today. She herself became a much revered style icon known for her simple yet sophisticated outfits worn with accessories like numerous strings of pearls. Coco was once quoted saying, "Luxury must be comfortable; otherwise it is not luxury."

Her early years, however, were anything but glamorous. She was born to an unwed mother, who worked as a laundry-woman. Her father was a peddler, who sold clothes and was always on the move. When Coco was 12, her mother died. After her mother's death, Coco's father sent her along with her two sisters to an orphanage while her two brothers were sent to work on a farm. She was raised by nuns who taught her how to sew—a skill that would lead to her life's work. She spent the next six years at the orphanage. When she was 18, she had to leave the orphanage as she was too old to live there. She then went to live in a boarding house and found herself work as a seamstress. While working thus, she also planned to make her career as a singer and so started singing cabaret in Vichy and Moulins. It was here while working as an aspiring singer that she took the name of Coco.

Fashion and Fragrance Pioneer

Around the age of 20, Coco became involved with Etienne Balsan, an ex-cavalry officer and a wealthy textile heir. She soon became his mistress and started living with him a life of luxury and indulgence. In 1908, Coco began an affair with one of Balsan's friends, Captain Arthur Edward 'Boy' Capel. Capel was a wealthy gentleman belonging to English upper class. He had Coco make her residence in an apartment in Paris. He also financed the first of Coco's stores. It is said that Capel's own sartorial style influenced the conception of the Chanel look. The bottle design for Chanel No. 5, Chanel's iconic perfume, is sometimes attributed to the sophisticated design sensibilities of Capel. It is believed that Coco adapted the rectangular, bevelled lines of the toiletry bottles that Capel carried in his travelling bag.

The couple spent time together at fashionable resorts such as Deauville. Coco hoped that they would perhaps settle down but even after an affair of nine years, a permanent settlement never came about. In 1919, Capel died in a car accident. His death served a great blow to Coco.

Opening her first shop on Paris's Rue Cambon in 1910, Coco started out selling hats. Her hats became a fashion statement after they were modeled and worn by theatre actress Gabrielle Dorziat. Coco later added stores in Deauville and Biarritz, and began making clothes. Her first taste of success for her clothing line came from a dress she had fashioned out of an old jersey. When people asked her where she had got the dress from, she replied by offering to make one for them. Soon, the clothes made by her were in great demand.

In the 1920s, Coco took her thriving business to new heights. She launched her first perfume, Chanel No. 5, which was the first to feature a designer's name. The fragrance was in fact also backed by department store owner Théophile Bader and businessmen Pierre and Paul Wertheimer, with Coco developing a close friendship with Pierre. A deal was ultimately negotiated where the

Wertheimer business would take in 70 percent of Chanel No. 5 profits for producing the perfume at their factories, with Bader receiving 20 percent and Coco herself only receiving 10 percent. The fragrance was loved enormously and hence for many years, Coco repeatedly sued the Wertheimers to have the terms of the deal renegotiated.

Suit and Little Black Dress

In 1925, Coco introduced the now legendary Chanel suit with collarless jacket and well-fitted skirt. Her designs were revolutionary for the time as she had borrowed elements from men's fashion to create her designs. While creating her designs, Coco put a lot of emphasis on comfort, which was a far cry from the fashion of the era. The clothes designed by her helped women say goodbye to the days of corsets and other confining garments.

Then in the 1920s, Coco brought forth a revolutionary design with Chanel's 'Little Black Dress'. In order to create her revolutionary design, she chose a colour once associated with mourning and she showed just how chic it could be for an evening wear. In addition to fashion, Coco was a popular figure in Parisian literary and artistic worlds as well. She had designed costumes for the Ballets Russes and Jean Cocteau's play Orphée, and counted Cocteau and artist Pablo Picasso among her friends.

Personal Life and Scandal

Another important romance for Chanel began in the 1920s. She met the wealthy duke of Westminster aboard his yacht around 1923. The two had a decade-long relationship. The duke even proposed marriage but Coco never complied.

On the business front, the international economic depression of the 1930s had a negative impact on her company. During World War II, Coco had to close down all her stores. During the German occupation of France, Coco got involved with a German military officer, Hans Gunther von Dincklage. She also got special permission to stay in his apartment at Hotel Ritz. After the war ended, Coco was interrogated for her relationship with von Dincklage.

While not officially charged, Coco suffered in the court of public opinion. Some still viewed her relationship with a Nazi officer as a betrayal of her country. Hearing the criticism, Coco left Paris and spent several years in Switzerland in what was considered a self-imposed exile. She also lived at her country house in Roquebrune for a time.

At the age of 70, Coco made a triumphant return to the fashion world. She first received scathing reviews from critics, but her feminine and easy-fitting designs soon won over shoppers around the world.

Legacy

In 1969, Coco's fascinating life story became the basis for the Broadway musical Coco, starring Katharine Hepburn as the legendary designer.

Coco died on January 10, 1971, at her apartment in Hotel Ritz. Hundreds came together at the Church of the Madeleine to bid farewell to the fashion icon. In tribute, many of the mourners wore Chanel suits.

A little more than a decade after her death, designer Karl Lagerfeld took the reins of her company to continue the Chanel legacy. Today, her namesake company is held privately by the

Wertheimer family and continues to thrive, believed to generate hundreds of millions in sales each year.

In addition to the longevity of her designs, Coco's life story continues to captivate people's attention. Several biographies have been written about the fashion revolutionary. She has also been portrayed both on screen and in theatre by reputed actresses.

Fast Facts

Chanel No. 5 was the first perfume ever to be named after its designer.

Hillary Clinton

Hillary Clinton was born Hillary Diane Rodham in Chicago, Illinois. Hillary is the eldest child of Hugh and Dorothy Rodham. She has two younger brothers.

As a young woman, Hillary was active in young Republican groups and campaigned for Republican presidential nominee Barry Goldwater in 1964. After attending a speech by Martin Luther King Jr., she decided to work for public welfare. She became a Democrat in 1968.

At Wellesley College, Hillary Clinton took keen interest in student politics. She graduated in 1969 and then attended Yale Law School, where she met Bill Clinton. After graduating with honours in 1973 from the law school, Hillary enrolled herself at the Yale Child Study Center. Here, she took courses on children and medicine, and completed one year of post-graduate study. During her summers as a college student, Hillary worked on a variety of jobs. In 1971, she first came to Washington, D.C. to work on U.S. Senator Walter Mondale's subcommittee on migrant workers. In the summer of 1972, she worked in the western states for the campaign of Democratic presidential nominee George McGovern.

In the spring of 1974, Hillary became a member of the presidential impeachment inquiry staff, advising the Judiciary Committee of the House of Representatives during the Watergate scandal. After President Richard M. Nixon resigned in August, she became a faculty member of the University of Arkansas School of Law, in Fayetteville.

Marriage to Bill Clinton

Hillary married Bill Clinton on October 11, 1975. In 1976, Hillary worked on Jimmy Carter's successful campaign for presidential election while her husband, Clinton, was elected attorney general of Arkansas at the age of 32. He was the youngest governor in the US. He held the same office from 1982 to 1988. Hillary joined the Rose Law Firm in Little Rock and in 1977, was appointed part-time chairman of the Legal Services Corporation by President Carter. While her husband served as the governor of Arkansas, Hillary chaired the Arkansas Educational Standards Committee, co-founded the Arkansas Advocates for Children and Families, and served on the boards of the Arkansas Children's Hospital, Legal Services and the Children's Defense Fund.

First Lady

During Clinton's 1992 presidential campaign, Hillary emerged as a dynamic and valued partner. Even after Clinton had won the elections, she did not indulge herself in the traditional role of the first lady. In 1993, Clinton selected her to head the Task Force on National Health Care Reform. But the reform never passed either of the two houses for it was too complicated and was thus abandoned in 1994.

Despite this failure, Hillary's involvement deepened her interest in health care, and taking cue from her past experience, she raised her voice concerning several issues related to children and family. In 1997, she was influential in the creation of the Children's Health Insurance Program. This programme provided funds to those

parents who were unable to pay for the health care of their children. She was also instrumental in the passing of the Adoption and Safe Families Act, a series of reforms aimed at American adoption and foster-care systems.

As first lady, Hillary also worked on various issues related to women. Working with attorney general Janet Reno, in 1995 she helped create the Violence Against Women office, and also travelled extensively to various nations to promote equal rights for women. But Hillary's tenure as first lady was not without its controversies. In 1993, she and her husband were implicated in a Department of Justice investigation relating to the Whitewater real estate project in Arkansas though she was never charged for the same.

Trouble arose again in 1998, when the White House became engulfed in the Monica Lewinsky scandal. Although Hillary publicly supported her husband during the ensuing fallout, she was reported to have considered leaving her husband. However, the U.S. Senate failed to convict Clinton and he completed his term as president.

Senate and First Presidential Bid

With her husband limited to two terms in the White House, Hillary was determined to seek the U.S. Senate seat from New York, held by outgoing Democrat Daniel Patrick Moynihan. Despite early problems, she won the seat by a wide

margin. When she was sworn in on January 3, 2001, Hillary became the first wife of a president to seek and win national office, and the first woman to be elected to the U.S. Senate from New York. In 2003, she also published a best-selling memoir, *Living History*.

In 2006, she won a second term in office. A year later, she announced her plan to run for the presidential elections. However, when she came up short, she extended her support to then-Senator Barack Obama. She campaigned hard to ensure the win of a Democrat in the

White House. Eventually, Obama was elected president of the United States in 2008.

U.S. Secretary of State

Shortly after winning the U.S. presidential election, Obama nominated Hillary as secretary of state. She accepted the nomination and became the 67th U.S. secretary of state on January 21, 2009.

During her tenure as secretary of state, Hillary used her position to make women's rights and human rights a central talking point of U.S. initiatives. She is also among the most travelled of all the secretaries in US history.

In the fight against terrorism, she was a strong supporter of President Obama in his decisions regarding military support for Afghanistan, and also for the use of American special forces in the assassination of Osama bin Laden in Pakistan.

However, following a controversy in 2012, she resigned from her post in 2013.

Bid for 2016 Presidency

After much speculation and assumptions over whether Hillary would run for the U.S. presidency, her plans were made official in the spring of 2015. On April 12, Hillary's campaign chairperson John D. Podesta announced via email that the former secretary of state was entering the race to secure the Democratic presidential nomination for the 2016 elections. Soon after, Hillary herself announced her bid for presidential elections. She is considered a front-runner and, if successful, would be the first woman to earn the nomination for a major party's presidential bid.

Fast Facts

In 1997, Hillary won a Grammy for Best Spoken Word Album for the audio of her book *It Takes a Village*.

Indira Gandhi

Indira Gandhi was the only child of Jawaharlal Nehru, the first prime minister of independent India. A stubborn but highly intelligent young woman, she enjoyed an excellent education in Swiss schools. She later enrolled herself at Vishva-Bharati University in Shantiniketan, India and at Somerville College, Oxford.

After her mother died in 1936, Indira became somewhat her father's hostess. She learnt to navigate complex relationships of diplomacy with some of the greatest leaders of the world. After completing her education, she joined the Congress Party in 1938.

In 1942, she married Feroze Gandhi, a fellow member of the party. The couple had two children, Sanjay and Rajiv. The Congress Party came to power when her father took office in 1947. She became a member of the party's working committee in 1955. In 1959, she was elected to the largely honorary post of party president. Five years later, she became member of the Rajya Sabha. The same year, in 1964, Lal Bahadur Shastri, the then prime minister, named her as the minister for information and broadcasting in his ministry. By now, Jawaharlal Nehru had passed away.

Political Career

In 1966, Lal Bahadur Shastri died of a heart attack and in an interesting turn of events, Indira was appointed the prime minister of India. Serving her term as prime minister, she surprised her father's old colleagues when she led the country with an iron hand, sacking some of the highest ranking officials. She also brought about a great change in agricultural programmes that improved the lot of her country's poor. For a time, she was hailed by the masses as a hero.

Diplomatic Success

In 1971, the Pakistani army conducted violent acts against the people of East Pakistan, resulting in nearly 10 million people fleeing to India. Indira then invited the Pakistani president to Shimla for a week-long summit. The two leaders eventually signed the Shimla Agreement, agreeing to solve the Kashmir issue by peaceful means. Indira's continuous work led to the creation of a new and independent nation of Bangladesh.

Indira also led a movement came to be known as the Green Revolution. In an effort to address the chronic food shortages that mainly affected the extremely poor Sikh farmers of Punjab region, Indira decided to increase crop diversification and food exports. She also led the way to create new job opportunities and a means to provide food to the people.

In March 1972, Indira again led her Congress Party to landslide victories in a number of elections to state legislative assemblies. However, shortly afterwards, her defeated Socialist Party opponent from the 1971 national election charged that she had violated the election laws. In June 1975, the High Court of Allahabad ruled against her, which meant that she would be deprived of her seat in the parliament and would be required to stay out of politics for six years. Her appeal to the Supreme Court brought no satisfactory result. She then took matters into her own hands and called for a state of emergency throughout India. Her political opponents were put into prison and she assumed all the emergency

powers. Many new laws were enacted that limited personal freedom. She also implemented several unpopular policies. The emergency was lifted two years later, in 1977.

Authoritarian Leanings and Imprisonment

Indira lost the next election and was later imprisoned. In 1980, her son Sanjay Gandhi, who had been serving as her chief political adviser, died in a plane crash in New Delhi. After Sanjay's death, Indira prepared her second son, Rajiv, for leadership.

Fall from Power and Return to Office

Public opposition to Indira's two years of emergency rule was vehement and widespread, and after it ended in early 1977, the released political rivals were determined to oust her and the new Congress Party from power. When long-postponed national parliamentary elections were held later in 1977, she and her party were soundly defeated. Morarji Desai became the new prime minister.

In early 1978 Indira and her supporters completed the split from the Congress Party by forming the Congress (I) Party—the 'I' signifying Indira. She later won a new seat in the Lok Sabha (lower chamber of the Indian Parliament) in November 1978 and her Congress (I) Party began to gather strength. Meanwhile, the government fell in August 1979. The elections that took place the next year led Indira to a sweeping victory.

As prime minister, Indira stuck to the quasi-socialist policies of industrial development that had been begun by her father. She established closer relations with the Soviet Union.

Assassination

During the early 1980s, Indira was faced with threats to the political integrity of India. Several states sought a larger measure of independence from the central government. Sikh separatists in the state of Punjab used violence to assert their demands for an autonomous state. In 1982, a large number of Sikhs, led by Sant Jarnail Singh Bhindranwale, occupied and fortified the Harmandir Sahib (Golden Temple) complex at Amritsar. Tensions between the government and the Sikhs escalated, and talks between the two parties came to no results. Eventually, in June 1984, Indira ordered the Indian army to attack and oust the separatists from the complex. Some buildings in the shrine were badly damaged in the fighting, and at least 450 Sikhs were killed. Five months later, Indira was killed in her garden in New Delhi in a succession of bullets fired by two of her own Sikh bodyguards in revenge for the attack in Amritsar. She died on her way to the hospital.

Fast Facts

As a child, Indira formed a group of kids called the 'monkey brigade' to spy on police and distributed Indian flags.

Madonna

Singer, performer and actress Madonna Louise Veronica Ciccone was born to Silvio 'Tony' Ciccone and Madonna Fortin. Her father worked as a defense engineer while her mother was an x-ray technician and a former dancer. The third of six children, Madonna learned early on how to handle her role as the middle child.

Her parents' strict observation of the Catholic faith played a large role in Madonna's childhood. Many elements of Catholic iconography later became the subject of Madonna's most controversial works.

Tragedy in Family

Madonna's mother had a significant influence on Madonna's early life. While she was pregnant with Madonna's youngest sister, her mother was diagnosed with breast cancer. Treatment had to be delayed until the baby reached full term, but by then the disease had grown too strong. On December 1, 1963, at the age of 30, Madonna's mother passed away. Madonna was only 5 years old at the time.

The loss of her mother significantly affected Madonna's adolescence. Around this time, Madonna was also determined to have her voice heard.

She fought hard against the rules imposed by her stepmother, Joan Gustafson. Gustafson would often make Madonna take care of the younger children in the household—a task that she greatly disliked. She then showed her rebellion by turning her conservative clothes into revealing outfits, rejecting her religious background and by frequently visiting the gay nightclubs.

Music and Dance

Madonna balanced this insubordinate side of her personality with a drive for perfectionism and high achievement. She was a top student at school, was a cheerleader and a disciplined dancer. She even graduated from high school a semester earlier than her peers. In 1976, her hard work earned her the attention of the University of Michigan. The university offered her full-time scholarship to their dance programme.

In 1977, during her undergraduate studies at Michigan, Madonna was awarded a six-week scholarship to study with the Alvin Ailey American Dance Theater in New York City. This was followed by a rare opportunity to perform with choreographer Pearl Lang in 1978. At the insistence of her dance instructor, the budding star dropped out of college after completing only two years of study. She then moved to New York to further her dance career.

In New York, Madonna paid her rent by doing a handful of odd jobs. In 1979, Madonna met Dan Gilroy, one of the founding members of a ska-influenced pop-punk band called Breakfast Club. Gilroy introduced Madonna to the head of a vaudeville review in Paris. During this trip she fell in love with the combination of singing and performing. She returned to the United States in 1980; soon after she joined Gilroy's band and became its lead singer.

Rise to Pop Stardom

In 1981, Madonna decided to go solo and hired manager Camille Barbone of Gotham Records to help her get her singing career on track. Camille helped Madonna put together a studio band that accentuated the budding star's hip

style. Friend Stephen Bray, a musician in her band, wrote her first hit, 'Everybody', which New York music producer Mark Kamins recorded. Kamins then helped Madonna score a record deal with Sire Records. 'Everybody' hit No. 1 in 1982.

Using the success of the song as leverage, Madonna convinced Sire to produce the full-length album, 'Madonna', in 1983. The album had a slow but steady success.

'Like a Virgin' was her follow-up album. The album hit No. 1 on the Billboard Chart. The title track later became listed as Madonna's biggest pop hit of all time. She had two other top 5 hits from the record: 'Material Girl' and the dance ditty with bounce, 'Angel'.

She also starred in her first mainstream feature film, *Desperately Seeking Susan* (1985), and performed the soundtrack single, 'Into the Groove', which hit No. 1 on the U.S. dance charts. She then started her first music tour, 'The Virgin Tour'. In time, 17 consecutive songs that she had sung and had written climbed to the Top 10 on the Billboard Chart. While her songs remained at the top, Madonna continued to reinvent her image.

In the next five years, Madonna's life was a whirlwind of activity. On August 16, 1985, she married actor Sean Penn and co-starred with him in the film *Shanghai Surprise* (1986). She then went on to star in three more movies over the next few years. She also released the hit albums: 'True Blue' (1986), 'Who's that Girl' (1987), 'You Can Dance' (1987), and 'Like a Prayer' (1989).

Shock Value

Madonna loved to mix her drive for success with her penchant for scandalous behaviour. Soon there was news of her marriage to Penn, which was marred by reports of domestic violence and later led to a very public divorce.

However, Madonna continued to enjoy her popularity among the masses. The album 'Like a Prayer' topped music charts. By 1991, she had achieved twenty-one Top 10 hits in the United States. Committed to controlling her career, she founded Maverick Records, a label under the Warner Music Group, in April 1992.

Personal Life

By 1996, Madonna had proven her versatility as a star in both films and music. She starred in the critically acclaimed screen adaptation of the Andrew Lloyd Webber musical *Evita* (1996). She won a Golden Globe for Best Performance by an Actress in a Motion Picture - Comedy or Musical. She performed 'You Must Love Me' in the movie, which earned her an Academy Award for Music, Original Song. In 1996, she gave birth to Lourdes Maria (Lola) Ciccone Leon, whom she had with her lover and personal trainer, Carlos Leon.

Years later, she released 'Something to

Remember' (1995), a round-up of her balladry that included the new song 'You'll See'. Again, in 1998, she released 'Ray of Light', a critically acclaimed outing that had her delving into electronica and spiritual exploration. More hits came in the form of songs like 'Frozen' and 'The Power of Good-Bye'. Madonna also earned three Grammys.

Next came 'Music' (2000), another successful electronic project. She continued her Grammy success with 'Beautiful Stranger', the soundtrack for Austin Powers: The Spy Who Shagged Me.

She reinvented herself as a mature and friendly Madonna after getting married to British director Guy Ritchie in 2000. She gave birth to a son, Rocco John Ritchie, the same year. She then made the move from the big screen to the London West End stage in the play Up for Grabs (2002), and wrote her first children's book, The English Roses. It was published in 2003, followed by the release of her album 'American Life'. Soon after, she and Ritchie announced their divorce after eight years of marriage.

Unrivalled Success

Despite facing setbacks in her personal life, her professional space continued to bloom. In January 2008, she was named the world's wealthiest female musician by Forbes magazine. Madonna earned much of this income from her H&M clothing line and a deal with NBC to air concert footage.

Tumultuous Road to 'Rebel Heart'

Through 2014, Madonna was reportedly at work on her next album. In December 2014, however, more than a dozen songs planned for her 2015 album 'Rebel Heart' were leaked online.

To counterattack the theft, Madonna released six songs online. In recent years, Madonna has continued to tour, release albums and engage in humanitarian work.

Fast Facts

The Guinness Book of World Records lists Madonna as the world's most successful female recording artist of all time, having sold over 200 million records worldwide.

Malala Yousafzai

Malala Yousafzai was born in Mingora, Pakistan. For the first few years of her life, her hometown remained a popular tourist spot that was known for its summer festivals. However, the area began to change as the Taliban tried to take control. She is the eldest of three siblings. Malala is fluent in Urdu, English and Pashto. She was mostly taught by her father who owns a chain of schools, is a poet and an educational activist himself.

Initial Activism

Yousafzai attended a school that her father, Ziauddin Yousafzai, had founded. After the Taliban began attacking girls' schools in Swat Valley, Malala decided to give a speech in Peshawar, Pakistan, in September 2008. The title of her talk was, 'How dare the Taliban take away my basic right to education?' The speech brought to light her thoughts about the Taliban's ban on the education of women. The speech had come in the wake of Taliban's destruction of several girls' schools in the region.

In early 2009, Malala started blogging for the BBC about living under the Taliban's threats to deny her an education. This blog was BBC's initiative to show the world how ordinary people lived and suffered under the threat of the Taliban. In order to hide her identity, she used the pseudonym Gul Makai. She would write the blog on a piece of paper, which was handed over to a reporter who would scan it and sent it to BBC.

However, she was revealed to be the BBC blogger in December the same year.

With a growing public platform, Malala continued to speak out about her right and the right of all women to an education. Her activism resulted in a nomination for the International Children's Peace Prize in 2011. The same year, she was awarded Pakistan's National Youth Peace Prize.

Targeted by the Taliban

When she was 14, Malala and her family learned that the Taliban had issued a death threat against her. Malala was afraid for the safety of her father, who was an anti-Taliban activist himself. The family also thought initially that the fundamentalist group would not actually harm a child. However, their notions were proved wrong when, on October 9, 2012, on her way home from school, a man boarded the bus Malala was riding in and demanded to know which girl was Malala. When her friends looked toward Malala, her location was given away. Without losing a moment, the gunman fired at her, hitting Malala in the left side of her head; the bullet then travelled down her neck and stopped only at her shoulder. Two other girls were also injured in the attack. But they were conscious enough to speak about the incident.

Malala, however, was in a critical condition and was flown to a military hospital in Peshawar. A portion of her skull was removed to treat her swelling brain. To receive further care, she was transferred to Birmingham, England.

Post-Attack

Once she was in the United Kingdom, Malala was taken out of a medically induced coma. Here, she also underwent multiple surgeries, including repair of a facial nerve to fix the paralyzed left side of her face. Surprisingly, she had suffered no brain damage. In March 2013, she was able to begin attending school in Birmingham.

The shooting resulted in a massive outpouring of support for Malala, which continued during her recovery. On her 16th birthday in 2013, she gave a speech at the United Nations. She has also written an autobiography, *I Am Malala: The Girl Who Stood Up for Education and Was Shot by the Taliban*, which was published in October 2013. Unfortunately, Malala continues to remain on the Taliban's hit list.

Despite the threats by the Taliban, Malala remains a staunch advocate for the power of education. On October 10, 2013, in acknowledgement of her work, the European Parliament awarded Malala the Sakharov Prize for Freedom of Thought. In 2013, she was nominated for the Nobel Peace Prize. She, however, only won it in March 2014. In August the same year, Leanin.org held a live chat on Facebook with Sheryl Sandberg and Malala about the importance of education for girls around the world. She talked about her story, her inspiration and family, her plans for the future and advocacy along with answering questions that social network users put forth.

In October 2014, Malala received the Nobel Peace Prize, along with Indian children's rights activist Kailash Satyarthi. At age 17, Malala became the youngest person to receive the Nobel Peace Prize. U.N. Secretary-General Ban Ki-moon described her as "a brave and gentle advocate of peace who through the

simple act of going to school became a global teacher."

On her 18th birthday on July 12, 2015, also called Malala Day, the young activist opened a school for Syrian refugee girls in Lebanon. This school was designed to admit girls aged 14 to 18 years.

That day, she also asked her supporters on The Malala Fund website: "Post a photo of yourself holding up your favourite book and share why YOU choose#BooksNotBullets - and tell world leaders to fund the real weapon for change, education!"

In October 2015, a documentary on Malala's life was released—*He Named Me Malala*. The documentary gave an insight into her life, family and her unbroken commitment to support education for girls around the world.

Fast Facts

The attack on Malala led Pakistan to create their first ever Right to Education Bill.

Malala has co-founded the Malala Fund, an organization that provides grants for the education of girls in countries like Pakistan, Nigeria, Kenya and Jordan.

She has received the International Children's Peace Prize, an Honorary Master of Arts from The University of Edinburgh, the Sakharov Prize for her bravery against the Taliban, the United Nations Human Rights Prize, and an honorary doctorate of civil law from University of King's College, amongst others.

Margaret Thatcher

Politician and former British Prime Minister Margaret Thatcher was born in Grantham, England. She was nicknamed the 'Iron Lady'. Her early education took place in Grantham. Her father owned a grocery store and the family lived in an apartment above the store. While still a young child, Margaret was first introduced to conservative politics by her father, who was a member of the town council.

Margaret was good at academics and managed to secure admission at the prestigious Oxford University after completing her schooling. Here, she studied chemistry at Somerville College. She remained politically active as president of the conservative association at the university. In 1947, she earned her degree in chemistry and then went on to work as a research chemist in Colchester. She continued her research in Dartford later on.

Early Foray into Politics

Two years after graduating from college, Margaret made her first bid for public office. In the 1950 elections, she ran as the conservative candidate for a Dartford parliamentary seat. She, however, knew that it would be difficult to win this seat from the liberal Labour Party. Nevertheless, her speeches earned her the respect of her political party peers. As she had predicted, she was defeated but she never lost hope. She tried again to win the seat but was again unsuccessful. It was somewhere around this time that she married Denis Thatcher.

In 1952, Margaret put politics aside for a time to study law. A year later, she and her husband welcomed twins Carol and Mark. Post delivery, Margaret continued her training in law and in 1953, she qualified as a barrister. However, she did not stay away from the political arena for too long. She won a seat in the House of Commons in 1959.

In no time, her political career took off. In 1961, Margaret was appointed parliamentary under secretary for pensions and national insurance. When the Labour Party came into power, she became a member of the Shadow Cabinet. It was a group of political leaders who would hold Cabinet-level posts if their party was in power.

Britain's First Female Premier

When Conservatives returned to office in June 1970, Margaret was appointed secretary of state for education and science. During this time, she was often called 'Thatcher, milk snatcher,' due to her abolition of the universal free school milk scheme. In this position, she had a difficult time, not only because of the bad press reviews that she received but also because she found it difficult to have the then prime minister Edward Heath listen to her ideas. She was apparently discouraged when she saw no future for women in politics. She was once quoted as saying during a television appearance in 1973, "I don't think there will be a woman prime minister in my lifetime."

Margaret soon proved herself wrong. While the Conservative Party lost power in 1974, she became a dominant force in her political party. She was elected leader of the Conservative Party in 1975. With this victory, Margaret became the first woman in the House of Commons to serve as the opposition leader. During this time, England was in a time of turmoil both economically and politically. The government was bankrupt, employment was on the rise and conflicts arose with labour unions. This instability helped the Conservatives to return to power in 1979. As party leader, Margaret made history in May 1979 when she became the first female British prime minister.

Conservative Leadership

As prime minister, Margaret battled the country's recession by initially raising interest rates to control inflation. She

was best known for her destruction of Britain's traditional industries. She achieved this through her attacks on labour organizations and by massive privatization of social housing and public transport. U.S. President Ronald Reagan, a fellow Conservative, was amongst her biggest allies at that moment. The two shared similar right-wing, pro-corporate political philosophies.

Margaret faced a military challenge during her first term. In April 1982, Argentina invaded the Falkland Islands. The islands were a disputed territory between the two nations as they were situated near the coast of Argentina. Taking swift action, Margaret sent British troops to the territory to retake the islands in what became known as the Falklands War. Argentina surrendered in June 1982.

Margaret was chosen for a second term as prime minister from 1983 to 1987. She handled a number of conflicts and crises during her second term, the most jarring of which may have been the assassination attempt on her in 1984. In a plot by the Irish Republic Army, she was meant to be killed by a bomb planted at the Conservative Conference in Brighton in October. Undaunted and unharmed, Margaret insisted that the conference should continue and it did. The next day, after the assassination attempt, she gave a speech at the conference.

As for foreign policy, Margaret met with Soviet leader Mikhail Gorbachev in 1984. The same year, she signed an agreement with the Chinese government concerning the future of Hong Kong. She also approved of Reagan's air raids on Libya in 1986, and even allowed U.S. forces to use British bases to carry out the attacks.

Resignation

Margaret returned for a third term in 1987. This time, she sought to implement a standard educational curriculum across the nation and make changes to the country's socialized medical system. She, however, lost support because of her efforts to implement a fixed rate local tax—a policy that led to massive protests across England and discontent within her party.

Margaret soon came under pressure from party members and resigned as prime minister.

Life After Politics

In 1992, Margaret was appointed to the House of Lords, as Baroness Thatcher of Kesteven. She wrote about her experiences as a world leader and a pioneering woman in the field of politics in two books: *The Downing Street Years* (1993) and *The Path to Power* (1995). In 2002, she published the book *Statecraft*, in which she shared her views on international politics.

Around this time, Margaret suffered a series of low-intensity strokes. She then suffered a great personal loss in 2003, when her husband, Denis, died. The following year, Margaret had to say goodbye to an old friend and ally, Ronald Reagan.

In 2005, Margaret celebrated her 80th birthday. A huge event was held in her honour and was attended by luminaries like Queen Elizabeth II, Tony Blair and nearly 600 other friends, family members and former colleagues.

Final Years and Legacy

Margaret's health made headlines in 2010, when she missed a celebration at 10 Downing Street, held in honour of her 85th birthday by David Cameron. Later, in November 2010, Margaret spent two weeks in the hospital. In 2011, she missed many major events and later in July 2011, her office was permanently closed. This was indicative of an end to her public life. Battling memory problems in her later years due to her strokes, Margaret retreated from the spotlight, living in near seclusion at her home in London's Belgravia neighbourhood.

Margaret died on April 8, 2013, at the age of 87. She was survived by her two children, daughter Carol and son Sir Mark. Margaret's policies and actions continue to be debated by detractors and supporters alike, showcasing the lasting impression that the illustrious lady had left on Britain and on nations worldwide.

Fast Facts

Margaret Thatcher became the first and only female prime minister of the United Kingdom. She was also the first prime minister with a science degree.

Mother Teresa

Catholic nun and missionary, Mother Teresa was born on August 26, 1910, in Skopje, present-day Republic of Macedonia. The following day, she was baptized as Agnes Gonxha Bojaxhiu. Her parents, Nikola and Dranafile Bojaxhiu, were Albanians. Her father was a construction contractor and a trader of medicines and other goods. Her family members were devoted Catholics.

In 1919, when Agnes was only 8 years old, her father suddenly fell ill and died. After her father's death, she became very close to her mother. Her mother was a pious and compassionate woman who taught her daughter to commit to doing charity.

Although by no means wealthy, Agnes extended an open invitation to the city's destitute to dine with her family.

Religious Calling

Young Agnes attended a convent-run primary school and then a state-run secondary school. As a girl, she sang in the local Sacred Heart choir and was often asked to sing solos. The congregation made an annual pilgrimage to the Church of the Black Madonna in Letnice. During one such trip, when she was 12 years old, she felt strongly the call of God. Six years later, in 1928, Agnes decided to join the Sisters of Loreto in Dublin, an Irish community of nuns with missions in India. Here, she soon took the name of Sister Mary Teresa after Saint Thérèse of Lisieux.

A year later, Sister Teresa travelled

to Darjeeling, India, for the novitiate period. In May 1931, she made her First Profession of Vows. Afterward she was sent to Calcutta (now Kolkata), where she was assigned to teach at Saint Mary's High School for Girls. It was a school run by the Loreto Sisters and was dedicated to teaching girls from the poorest Bengali families in the city. While in Calcutta, Sister Teresa learned to speak both Bengali and Hindi fluently as she taught geography and history. She had now dedicated her life to alleviate the girls' poverty by educating them.

On May 24, 1937, she took her Final Profession of Vows to a life of poverty, chastity and obedience. Then, as was the custom with Loreto nuns, she took on the title of 'Mother' upon making her final vows and came to be known as Mother Teresa. She continued to teach at Saint Mary's, and in 1944 became the principal of the school. Through her kindness, generosity and unfailing commitment to her students' education, she sought to lead them to a life of devotion to Christ.

A New Calling

However, on September 10, 1946, Mother Teresa experienced a second calling. It was a "call within a call" that changed her life forever. She was riding a train from Calcutta to the Himalayan foothills for a retreat when Jesus Christ spoke to her and told her to abandon teaching and work in the slums of Calcutta; she was also asked to provide aid to the poorest and sickest people in the city.

Since Mother Teresa had taken a vow of obedience, she could not leave her convent without official permission. It took her more than a year to get approval from local Archbishop Ferdinand Périer to pursue her new calling. In August 1948, wearing the blue-and-white sari that she would always wear

in public for the rest of her life, she left the Loreto Convent and went out into the city. After six months of basic medical training, she voyaged for the first time into Calcutta's slums with no more specific goal than to aid "the unwanted, the unloved, the uncared for."

The Missionaries of Charity

Mother Teresa quickly translated this somewhat vague calling into concrete action in order to help the city's poor. She began an open-air school and established a home for the dying and the destitute in a dilapidated building, which she managed to convince the city government to donate her for the cause.

In October 1950, she won canonical recognition for a new congregation, the Missionaries of Charity, which she founded with only a handful of members. These members were some of the people that she knew.

As the ranks of her congregation swelled and donations poured in from around India and across the globe, the charities that Mother Teresa could do increased. During the 1950s and 60s, she established a leper colony, an orphanage, a nursing home along with a family clinic, and a string of mobile health clinics.

In 1971, Mother Teresa travelled to New York City to open her first American-

based house of charity. In the summer of 1982, she flew secretly to Beirut, Lebanon, where she crossed between Christian East Beirut and Muslim West Beirut to aid children of both faiths. In 1985, Mother Teresa returned to New York and spoke at the 40th anniversary of the United Nations General Assembly. While there, she also opened Gift of Love, a home to care for those infected with HIV/AIDS.

International Charity and Recognition

In February 1965, Pope Paul VI bestowed the Decree of Praise upon the Missionaries of Charity. This praise prompted Mother Teresa to expand the Missionaries of Charity internationally. By 1997, the Missionaries of Charity had 4000 foundations in 123 countries across the globe.

The Decree of Praise, bestowed on her by the Pope, was just the beginning, as Mother Teresa received various honours for her tireless and effective charity. She was awarded the Jewel of India, one of the highest Indian diasporic awards granted annually to non-resident persons of Indian origin, as well as the now-defunct Soviet Union's Gold Medal of the Soviet Peace Committee. In 1979, Mother Teresa won her highest honour when she received the Nobel Peace Prize in recognition of her work "in bringing help to suffering humanity."

Controversy

Despite this widespread praise, Mother Teresa's life and work have not gone without criticism. In particular, she has drawn criticism for her vocal endorsement of some of the Catholic Church's more controversial doctrines, such as opposition to contraception and abortion.

Death and Legacy

After several years of deteriorating health, Mother Teresa died on September 5, 1997, at the age of 87. She was beatified in October 2003 by the papacy.

Since her death, Mother Teresa has remained in the public spotlight. In particular, the publication of her private correspondence in 2003 caused a wholesale re-evaluation of her life by revealing the crisis of faith she suffered for almost the last 50 years of her life.

For her unwavering commitment to aiding those most in need, Mother Teresa stands out as one of the greatest humanitarians of the 20th century. She combined profound empathy and a fervent commitment to look after and provide for the poorest of the poor.

Fast Facts

Mother Teresa once traveled through a war zone to rescue 37 children from the front lines.

Oprah Winfrey

American television host, actress, producer, philanthropist and entrepreneur Oprah Gail Winfrey was born in Kosciusko, Mississippi. She had a troubled childhood in a small farming community. While still a child, she was abused by some of her male relatives. Eventually, her mother Vernita moved to Nashville and unable to support Oprah, she sent her to live with her father, Vernon, a barber and businessman. Her father was strict but encouraged her in her education. Oprah then completed her education and later entered Tennessee State University in 1971. While still at the university, she began working in radio and television broadcasting in Nashville.

In 1976, Oprah moved to Baltimore, Maryland, where she hosted the TV chat show *People Are Talking*. The show, which initially had a low rating, had turned into a huge hit after Oprah started off as a host. She worked on the show for eight years until she was recruited by a Chicago TV station to host her own morning show, *A.M. Chicago*. Her major competitor in the time slot was Phil Donahue. Within several months, Oprah's open, warm-hearted personal style had won her 100,000 more viewers than Donahue and had catapulted her show ratings to the first in the race. Her success brought her recognition and fame along with a role in Steven Spielberg's 1985 film, *The Color Purple*. Oprah won a nomination for Best Supporting Actress for her performance in the film.

Oprah launched the Oprah Winfrey Show

in 1986 as a nationally syndicated programme. With its placement on 120 channels and an audience of 10 million people, the show grossed US$ 125 million by the end of its first year. Oprah received US$ 30 million out of the total amount. She soon gained ownership of the programme from ABC, drawing it under the control of her new production company, Harpo Productions, which is Oprah spelled backwards.

Success and Fame

In 1994, while talk shows discussed tabloid topics, Oprah did no such thing. As a result, she initially lost her audience but she soon earned the respect of her viewers and was rewarded with an upsurge in popularity. Her projects with Harpo have included the highly rated 1989 TV mini-series, *The Women of Brewster Place*, which she also starred in. She also signed a multi-picture contract with Disney.

Oprah gained as much recognition for her weight loss efforts as for her talk show, and later competed in the Marine Corps Marathon in Washington, D.C., in 1995. In the wake of her highly publicized success, her personal chef, Rosie Daley, and trainer, Bob Greene, both published best-selling books.

Oprah then launched her 'Oprah's Book Club', as part of her talk show. The programme propelled many unknown authors to the top of the bestseller lists and gave 'pleasure reading' a new kind of prominence.

With the debut in 1999 of Oxygen Media, a company she co-founded for producing cable and Internet programming for women, Oprah secured her place in the forefront of the media industry and as one of the most powerful and

wealthy people in show business. In 2002, she concluded a deal with the network to air a prime-time complement to her syndicated talk show. Her highly successful monthly magazine, *The Oprah Magazine*, debuted in 2000, and in 2004, she signed a new contract to continue *The Oprah Winfrey* Show through the 2010–11 season. Her show was seen in more than a 100 countries worldwide.

The Oprah Winfrey Network

In 2009, Oprah announced the close of her programme when her contract with ABC ended. Soon after, she moved to her own network, the Oprah Winfrey Network, a joint venture with Discovery Communications.

Despite a financially rocky start, the network made headlines in January 2013, when it aired an interview between Winfrey and Lance Armstrong, the American cyclist and seven-time Tour de France winner.

In March 2015, Oprah announced that her Chicago-based Harpo Studios would close at the end of the year to consolidate the company's production operations to the Los Angeles-based OWN headquarters. Oprah's television empire was launched at the studio and it had been home to her daily syndicated talk show through its finale in 2011.

Activism and Charity

According to *Forbes* magazine, Oprah was the richest African-American of the 20th century and the world's only Black billionaire for three years running. *Life* magazine hailed her as the most influential woman of her generation. In 2005, *Business Week* named her the greatest Black philanthropist in American history. Oprah's Angel Network has raised more

than US$ 51,000,000 for charitable programmes, including girls' education in South Africa and relief to the victims of Hurricane Katrina.

Besides being a philanthropist, Oprah has also been a dedicated activist for children's rights. In 1994, President Clinton signed a bill into law that Oprah had proposed to Congress, creating a nationwide database of convicted child abusers. She founded the *Family for Better Lives Foundation* and also contributes to her alma mater, Tennessee State University. In September 2002, Oprah was named the first recipient of the Academy of Television Arts & Sciences' Bob Hope Humanitarian Award.

Oprah campaigned for Barack Obama in December 2007, attracting a large congregation of people. This was the first time that she had campaigned for any political candidate.

Fast Facts

In what can be called Oprah's first, she joined Obama for a series of rallies in the early primary/caucus states of Iowa, New Hampshire, and South Carolina. It was the first time that she had ever campaigned for a political candidate.

In 2013, Oprah was awarded the Presidential Medal of Freedom (the nation's highest civilian honour) by President Barack Obama.

In November 2013, she received the nation's highest civilian honour, the Presidential Medal of Freedom, from President Barack Obama for her contributions to the country.

Princess Diana

Princess Diana was born on July 1, 1961 at Park House near Sandringham, Norfolk. She was the third of four children of John Spencer, Viscount Althorp, and his first wife, Frances. The Spencers had been closely allied with the Royal Family for several generations. Lady Diana's parents separated in 1967 and her father later married Raine, Countess of Dartmouth in 1976.

Together with her two elder sisters Sarah, Jane and her younger brother Charles, Diana continued to live with her father at Park House, Sandringham, which was owned by Queen Elizabeth II. During her stay there, Diana became acquainted with the Queen's youngest sons, Prince Andrew and Prince Edward.

Diana became known as Lady Diana Spencer after her father inherited the title of Earl Spencer in 1975. Diana was often noted for her shyness while growing up, but she did take keen interest in both music and dance, and was trained in classical ballet.

Education and Career

In 1968, Diana was sent to Riddlesworth Hall School, an all-girls boarding school. While she was young, she attended a local public school. She did not shine academically, and was moved to West Heath Girls' School in Sevenoaks, Kent. Here too, she performed poorly. However, she showed a particular talent as an accomplished pianist. Her outstanding community spirit was recognized with an award from West Heath. In 1977, she left

Hall of Fame

Angela Merkel
Chancellor

Coco Chanel
Fashion Designer

Hillary Clinton
Politician

Indira Gandhi
Prime Minister

Madonna
Singer, Actress

Malala Yousefani
Student, Humanitarian

Margaret Thatcher
Prime Minister

Mother Teresa
Missionary

Oprah Winfrey
Talk Show Host

Princess Diana
Princess

Serena Williams
Tennis Player

Fast Facts
She is the only tennis player to ever accomplish a golden career grand slam in singles and doubles.

Charity Work

As part of the Serena Williams Foundation's work, Serena has helped to fund the construction of the Serena Williams Secondary School in Matooni, Kenya. Through her foundation, she also provides under-privileged students in the United States with university scholarships. She also works with various community centres, particularly those that focus on the youth. Serena, along with her sister Venus, is a supporter and contributor of First Serve Miami, a foundation for youth who want to learn tennis but do not have the funds to support their love for the sport. She has been an International Goodwill Ambassador with UNICEF since 2011 and has helped launch UNICEF's Schools for Asia campaign. Along with these initiatives, she also supports a number of other foundations.

become the oldest Grand Slam singles champion in the Open era.

Personal Life

Besides tennis, Serena has interests in film, television and fashion. She has developed her own 'Aneres' line of clothing. In 2002, *People* magazine selected her as one of its 25 Most Intriguing People. She has also made television appearances and lent her voice to shows like *The Simpsons*.

She has also formed the Serena Williams Foundation and built schools in Africa in her efforts to do something for the under-privileged students. She is also the first African-American who, along with her sister, owns part of an NFL team.

Playing Style

Serena is a baseline player who immediately takes control of the game with her powerful serve. She returns the serve forcefully from both her forehand and backhand swings. Her forehand is considered to be among the most powerful shots in the women's game. She is an aggressive player who plays a 'high risk' style. Her favourite surface to play on is clay as she gets extra time to set up her shot. Serena is considered by many, including commentators, players and writers alike, as the greatest female tennis player of all times. She has won 36 major titles, which include 21 singles titles and 13 women's doubles.

defeating her sister Venus in the finals of each of these tournaments. She secured her first Australian Open in 2003, becoming the second woman (after Steffi Graf) to win a career Grand Slam. Her dream to win all the four grand slams simultaneously, which she had dubbed as 'The Serena Slam,' was now fulfilled. In 2008, she won the U.S. Open and later with her sister, Venus, won the second women's doubles Olympic gold medal at the Beijing Olympics.

In 2008, she landed herself in a controversy during the U.S. Open. She was heavily fined and was also put under probation. However, she returned with a bang in 2009 and won the Australian Open and Wimbledon, in both the singles and doubles category. The same year, she also released her autobiography, *Queen of the Court*.

In 2011, due to some severe health issues, Serena was sidelined from tennis for a few months. She, however, quickly recovered and was her dominant self in the U.S. Open but she lost in the finals. Serena again stumbled badly at the 2012 French Open, where she crashed out of the tournament in the first round itself. But she was back in top form in London, where she went on to win her fifth Wimbledon title. It was the first major title that she had won in almost two years.

At the 2012 Summer Olympics, she won the gold medal in the women's singles and won the doubles gold with her sister Venus. Later that year, she even won the U.S. Open. Her winning streak continued into the next year and the year after that.

By the summer of 2015, she had won 20 singles titles that ranked her third in the all-time best. "When I was a little girl, in California, my father and my mother wanted me to play tennis," she told the crowd in French after her victory. "And now, I'm here with 20 Grand Slam titles." By winning Wimbledon 2015, she has

Serena Williams

The youngest of Richard and Oracene Williams' five daughters, Serena Williams, along with her sister Venus, became one of the greatest champions in the field of tennis.

Serena's father—a former sharecropper from Louisiana determined to see his two youngest girls succeed—used what he had learned from tennis books and videos to instruct Serena and Venus on how to play the game. At the age of 3, the two girls started practicing rigorously for two hours daily. The girls played on courts that were replete with potholes and sometimes missing nets. Both Serena and Venus cut their teeth on the game of tennis and the requirements for persevering in a tough climate.

By 1991, Serena was 46-3 on the junior United States Tennis Association tour, and ranked first in the 10-and-under division. By this time, the family also moved to Florida. There, Serena's father let go of some of his coaching responsibilities, but continued to manage both his daughters' careers.

Rise of a Tennis Star

In 1995, Serena turned to professional tennis. Four years later, and with a lot of hard work, she won her first Grand Slam by winning the 1999 U.S. Open singles title. It set the stage for a run of high-powered, high-profile victories for both the Williams sisters. With their signature style and play, their sheer power and athletic ability, the two sisters overwhelmed their opponents.

In 2002, Serena won the French Open, the U.S. Open, and Wimbledon by

during her funeral procession. The funeral was held at Westminster Abbey, and was broadcasted on television. Her body was later buried at her family's estate, Althorp.

In 2007, marking the tenth anniversary of her death, her sons, Prince William and Prince Harry, honoured their beloved mother with a special concert that was held on what would have been her 46th birthday. The proceeds of the event went to charities supported by Diana and her sons.

Continuing her charitable efforts is the Diana, Princess of Wales Memorial Fund. Established after her death, the fund provides grants to numerous organizations and supports initiatives to provide care to the sick in Africa, help refugees and stop the use of landmines.

Fast Facts

Princess Diana supported over 100 charities, including the International Campaign to Ban Landmines, which won her the Nobel Peace Prize a few months after her death.

The Diana Award is awarded to courageous, caring, compassionate young people, transforming the lives of others in the name of Diana, Princess of Wales.

not meant to stay for long. The two became estranged over the years, and there were reports of infidelity from both parties. Finally, the couple announced their separation in December 1992. The separation statement was announced by British Prime Minister John Major to the House of Commons. However, their divorce was finalized in 1996.

Death and Legacy

Even after the divorce, Diana continued to remain popular in the royal household. She devoted herself to her sons and to charitable efforts like the battle against the use of landmines. She used her international celebrity status to help raise awareness about this issue and the disastrous effects of landmines. She also continued to experience the negative aspects of fame; her passionate romance with Egyptian film producer and playboy Dodi Al-Fayed caused quite a stir. The media was in a state of frenzy. While visiting Paris, the couple was involved in a car crash after trying to escape the paparazzi on the night of August 30, 1997.

Diana initially survived the crash but only a few hours later, she lost her battle with the injuries and died in a Paris hospital. Al-Fayed and the driver were also killed in the crash, while a bodyguard was seriously injured.

News of Diana's sudden death shocked the world. Thousands turned out to pay tribute to the "people's princess"

West Heath and briefly attended Institute Alpin Videmanette, a finishing school in Rougemont, Switzerland. Around the same time, she became reacquainted with her future husband, who was in a relationship with her older sister, Sarah. Diana wanted to be a professional ballerina with the Royal Ballet. She even studied ballet and tap dance in her childhood and teenage years. However, she never became a ballerina. After leaving Institut Alpin Videmanette, she moved to London in 1978.

In London, Diana lived in her mother's flat. Soon afterwards, an apartment at Coleherne Court in Earls Court was purchased by her mother as Diana's 18th birthday present. She lived there until 25 February 1981. Later, while working as a kindergarten assistant at the Young England Kindergarten, Pimlico, she became famous as the new girlfriend of Prince Charles, the heir to the British throne who was 13 years her senior.

Prince Charles was usually the subject of media attention and his courtship of Diana was no exception. The press was fascinated by the odd couple where the prince was reserved while the princess was a shy young woman with interest in fashion and popular culture. The couple got married on July 29, 1981 at St. Paul's Cathedral. The ceremony was broadcasted on television around the world, with millions of people tuning in to see what many considered a fairy-tale wedding. She was the first Englishwoman to marry the heir to the throne in 300 years.

Marriage and Divorce

On June 21, 1982, Diana and Charles had their first child: Prince William Arthur Philip Louis. He was joined by a brother, Prince Henry Charles Albert David—known widely as Prince Harry—more than two years later on September 15, 1984. After fulfilling her royal duties for a while and after being in continuous spotlight for a while, Diana began to develop and pursue her own interests. She worked for and supported many charitable organizations. She worked relentlessly for the homeless, for people living with HIV and AIDS, and for children in need.

Unfortunately, the fairy tale wedding of Princess Diana and Prince Charles was

41